Creating a
Traditional
Christmas

Creating a Traditional Christmas

TED SMART

This edition produced for The Book People Ltd
Hall Wood Avenue, Haydock, St Helens WA11 9UL

First published in 2002 by
New Holland Publishers (UK) Ltd
London • Cape Town • Sydney • Auckland
www.newhollandpublishers.com

Garfield House, 86-88 Edgware Road, London W2 2EA
United Kingdom

80 McKenzie Street, Cape Town 8001, South Africa

Level 1, Unit 4, 14 Aquatic Drive, Frenchs Forest, NSW 2086
Australia

218 Lake Road, Northcote, Auckland, New Zealand

10 9 8 7 6 5 4 3 2 1

Co-ordinating Editor: Emily Preece-Morrison
Designers: Bridgewater Book Company
Contributors: Premier Milling, Carol Deacon, Juliet Bawden,
Coral Walker, Vivienne Bolton, Labeena Ishaque, Janice
Murfitt, Ann Nicol, Stephanie Donaldson, Lynda Watts,
David Biggs, Susan Berry
Photographers: Edward Allwright, Shona Wood, Chris Turner,
Kulbir Thandi, Janine Hosegood, Willie van Heerden,
Jan Baldwin, Viv Yeo, Ryno
Production: Hazel Kirkman
Editorial Direction: Rosemary Wilkinson

Reproduction by Modern Age Repro House Ltd, Hong Kong
Printed and bound by Times Offset (M) Sdn. Bhd., Malaysia

Note: Use either metric or imperial measurements
in any one recipe, but do not mix the two.

CONTENTS

Christmas Food and Drink 6

Traditional Treats

Winter Warmers

Christmas Decorations 28

Christmas Cards 44

The Christmas Table 56

Christmas Food and Drink

Christmas is a time for feasting and indulgence.

There are so many traditional recipes to make during

the festive season, your kitchen will be bursting with

delicious treats. Cakes, biscuits and pies also make

useful presents. Always keep some popular goodies and

some warming winter drinks on stand-by to offer those

guests who inevitably drop by unannounced.

Christmas cakes & biscuits

A moist, fruity Christmas cake is essential for any festive celebration. Rich fruit cakes should be made at least two months before Christmas to allow all the flavours to develop. Sprinkle a little brandy over cakes once a month to keep them moist. If you make smaller, individual cakes, they make ideal gifts, as do decorated Christmas tree biscuits.

YOU WILL NEED

125 g (4 oz) margarine
125 g (4 oz) caster sugar
1 tsp vanilla extract
1 egg
280 g (9 oz) plain flour
4 tbsp cornflour
1 tsp baking powder
½ tsp salt
silver balls and sprinkles, to decorate
narrow ribbon, to hang

ICING

180 g (6 oz) icing sugar
about 2 tbsp boiling water
½ tsp vanilla extract or lemon juice

Christmas tree biscuits

1 Preheat oven to 180°C (350°F/gas mark 4). Beat margarine and sugar together. Add vanilla extract and egg and beat until light and fluffy.

2 Sift dry ingredients, add to creamed mixture and knead to form a stiff dough.

3 Roll out to a thickness of 3 mm (⅛ in) and, using a Christmas biscuit cutter, cut into shapes. For hanging the biscuits from a tree, make a hole for the ribbon with an icing nozzle.

4 Place on a greased baking tray and bake in the preheated oven for 10-15 minutes, or until light brown at the edges.

5 Remove biscuits from tray using a spatula; place on a wire rack to cool.

6 To make icing, sift icing sugar and add enough boiling water to make a smooth consistency. Add vanilla extract or juice to flavour.

7 Ice biscuits and decorate with silver balls, and so on. Thread ribbon through the hole and tie to the tree.

500g (1 lb) mixed dried fruit
110g (3½ oz) glacé cherries, halved
250 g (8 oz) sugar
90 g (3 oz) butter or margarine
250 ml (8 fl oz) water
280 g (9 oz) plain flour
2 tsp bicarbonate of soda
½ tsp salt
1 egg, beaten
4 tbsp brandy

boiled fruit cake

1 Preheat oven to 150°C (300°F/gas mark 2). Boil dried fruit, cherries, sugar, butter or margarine and water together for about 10 minutes. Leave to cool.

2 Sift the flour, bicarbonate of soda and salt together and stir well into the fruit mixture.

3 Mix in beaten egg and brandy. Line a 20 cm (8 inch) round, loose-bottomed cake tin with two layers brown paper or two layers greaseproof paper. Grease well and turn mixture into tin.

4 Bake in the preheated oven for 1¼ hours. Test centre of cake with a skewer. If baked, skewer will come out clean. Leave in turned-off oven for a while to prevent sinking. Remove from oven.

5 Allow to cool completely in tin before turning out. Sprinkle with brandy and seal. Allow to mature for at least 2 weeks.

YOU WILL NEED

725 g (1½ lb) mixed dried fruit

125 g (4 oz) stoned dates, finely chopped

210 g (7 oz) glacé cherries, halved

60 g (2 oz) pecan nuts or walnuts, chopped

125 ml (4 fl oz) brandy

250 g (8 oz) butter

180 g (6 oz) brown sugar

5 eggs

1 tbsp sieved apricot jam

280 g (9 oz) plain flour

pinch of salt

½ tsp ground nutmeg

½ tsp ground cinnamon

1 tsp mixed spice

1 tsp ground ginger

½ tsp ground cloves

½ tsp bicarbonate of soda

ICING

marzipan

sugarpaste (rolled fondant icing)

Tip

If the top of your fruit cake is a little too crusty for your taste, cover it with a layer of sliced raw apple. Leave in an airtight container for 24 hours. After a day the crust will become soft and moist and the apple slices can be removed.

CLOCKWISE FROM TOP:
Christmas Tree Biscuits, Boiled Fruit Cake and Moist Christmas Cake.

moist Christmas cake

1 Preheat oven to 150°C (300°F/gas mark 2). Mix dried fruit, dates, cherries, nuts and brandy together and leave overnight.

2 Cream butter and sugar together and add eggs; beat well after each addition until light and fluffy. Add jam and fruit mixture, mixing well.

3 Add sifted dry ingredients and mix well.

4 Line a 20 cm (8 in) square cake tin with two layers brown paper or two layers greaseproof paper. Grease well, turn mixture into tin and level top of cake mixture with spatula. Bake in the preheated oven for 2½ hours.

5 Test centre of cake with a skewer. If baked, skewer will come out clean.

6 Allow to cool completely in tin. Turn out and remove lining. Sprinkle with brandy; seal with cling film.

7 Store in a cool place. Sprinkle a little brandy over cake once a month to keep it moist.

8 Spread thin layer of jam over entire cake. Cover with marzipan and ice with rolled fondant icing.

Christmas puddings & pies

No Christmas meal is complete without a delicious steamed pudding smothered in brandy sauce. Pop some coins covered in foil into the mix for a surprise treat. You can spread some Yuletide cheer by making large batches of mincepies and giving them to your friends and family. They are also ideal to offer those last-minute, unexpected guests.

YOU WILL NEED

180 g (6 oz) raisins

250 ml (8 fl oz) brandy or sherry

250 g (8 oz) butter

250 g (8 oz) sugar

4 eggs

150 g (5 oz) plain flour

2 tsp bicarbonate of soda

½ tsp salt

2 tsp ground cinnamon

½ tsp ground ginger

½ tsp ground nutmeg

½ tsp allspice

150 g (5 oz) stoned dates, chopped

150 g (5 oz) currants

125 g (4 oz) pecan nuts, chopped

125 g (4 oz) raw carrot, finely grated

60 g (2 oz) fresh breadcrumbs

3 tbsp golden syrup

1 tbsp grated lemon rind

1 tbsp grated orange rind

SERVES 8–10

traditional Christmas pudding

1 Soak raisins in brandy or sherry overnight.

2 Beat butter and sugar together. Add eggs, one at a time, beating well after each addition.

3 Sift dry ingredients together, add to creamed mixture, and mix well. Add remaining ingredients and raisins.

4 Spoon mixture into a greased 2 litre (3 pints) metal pudding bowl. Cover with a double layer of foil or greaseproof paper and secure with string or a metal top.

5 Place on a wire rack in a large saucepan and pour in boiling water, to reach halfway up sides of bowl.

6 Steam for 2½-3 hours, or until well cooked, remembering to check water level and refill if necessary.

7 Allow to stand in bowl for at least 20 minutes before turning out.

8 Serve hot with brandy sauce or cream.

Tips

To re-heat, steam pudding for 30 minutes as directed in the recipe.

Place a tea towel over the top of the bowl before placing the lid on the saucepan, as this absorbs the condensation and prevents the pudding from going soggy.

CLOCKWISE FROM TOP RIGHT:
Traditional Christmas Pudding,
Christmas Mincemeat Slices
and Mince Pies.

30 g (1 oz) butter

250 g (8 oz) caster sugar

3 tbsp brandy

2 eggs, separated

125 ml(4 fl oz) single cream
or milk

brandy sauce

1 Using a double boiler, melt butter while gradually beating in sugar.

2 Add brandy, beat well, add egg yolks, and cream or milk.

3 Cook until thickened.

4 Beat egg whites and fold in lightly until smooth. Serve hot.

---

280 g (9 oz) plain flour

½ tsp salt

180 g (6 oz) cold butter

1 tbsp caster sugar

1 egg, separated

4 tsp iced water

1 tsp lemon juice

440 g (14 oz) jar fruit mincemeat

caster sugar, for sprinkling

MAKES **16**

Tip

Place a small piece of unsalted butter in fruit pies to prevent juice from running out when baking.

mince pies

1 Sift flour and salt together. Cut butter into small pieces and rub into flour with fingertips until mixture resembles breadcrumbs.

2 Mix in sugar. Mix egg yolk, water and lemon juice into dry ingredients to make a stiff dough. Knead well.

3 Wrap pastry dough in cling film and chill in refrigerator for about 1 hour.

4 Roll out pastry to a thickness of 3 mm (⅛ in). Cut out rounds to fit base of patty pans or bun tins. Cut the same number of smaller circles to form the lids of mincepies.

5 Place 1 tsp fruit mincemeat on the base of each pastry round.

6 Dampen pastry edge with water, cover with pastry lid, and seal. Prick holes in the lid with a fork or make a small incision with the tip of a sharp knife. Brush with lightly beaten egg white or iced water.

7 Bake in a preheated oven at 200°C (400°F/ gas mark 6) for 15 minutes, or until golden brown. Sprinkle with caster sugar while still warm.

---

125 g (4 oz) margarine

3 tbsp caster sugar

5 tsp oil

1 egg

1 tsp vanilla extract

280 g (9 oz) plain flour

2 tsp baking powder

pinch of salt

440 g (14 oz) jar fruit mincemeat

1 apple, peeled and grated

5 tbsp brandy

icing sugar, for dusting

MAKES **12**

Christmas mince pie slices

1 Cream margarine and sugar well.

2 Add oil, egg and vanilla extract, and beat well together.

3 Sift dry ingredients together and knead into creamed mixture to form a dough.

4 Press half of dough into a greased 23 cm (9 in) round ovenproof dish.

5 Mix fruit mincemeat, apple and brandy together and spread thickly over dough.

6 Coarsely grate remaining dough over mincemeat.

7 Bake in a preheated oven at 180°C (350°F/gas mark 4) for 20 minutes, or until golden brown.

8 Dust with icing sugar before slicing.

Festive favourites

In medieval times, Twelfth Night was a night for games, feasting and masques and traditionally marked the end of the Christmas celebrations. Today, a Twelfth Night cake is a delicious way to end the season of indulgence. A more modern alternative, which children especially love, is a chocolatey yule log. Decorate it with tiny feathered robin decorations and holly to make a merry winter scene.

twelfth night cake

1 Preheat the oven to 160°C (325°F/gas mark 3). Grease and line a 20 cm (8 in) round deep cake tin.

2 Cream the fat and sugar together until light and fluffy. Sift in the flour, baking powder and ground almonds, add the evaporated milk and fold together. Whisk the egg whites until stiff, then fold into the mixture with the fruits and nuts.

3 Spoon the mixture into the tin and level the top. Bake in preheated oven for about 1½ hours or until firm to the touch in the centre. Leave to cool in the tin for about 5 minutes, then turn out onto a wire rack to cool completely.

4 Brush the top of the cake with sieved apricot jam and press over crystallized fruits in a pattern.

chocolate yule log

1 Preheat the oven to 220°C (425°F/gas mark 7). Oil and line a 23 x 33 cm (9 x 13 in) Swiss roll tin with oiled greaseproof paper.

2 Sift together the flour, cocoa and salt.

3 Place the eggs and sugar in a large heatproof bowl and set over a pan of hot water. Whisk until thick, remove from the hot water and continue whisking until the mixture is very thick and pale and firm enough to leave a ribbon trail when the whisk is lifted. Fold in half the flour mixture. Fold in the remaining flour with 1 tbsp hot water.

4 Pour the mixture into the prepared tin and spread evenly. Bake in preheated oven for about 10 minutes or until firm to the touch.

5 Have ready a dampened tea towel spread out flat and a large sheet of greaseproof paper on top of it, dusted with caster sugar. Turn out the sponge on to the paper, peel away the lining paper and trim the edges with a sharp knife. Loosely roll up the sponge, rolling the sugared

paper inside. Leave the cake to cool, keeping it in a nicely rounded shape.

6 To make chocolate buttercream, cream the butter until very soft. Beat in the sugar a little at a time, then beat in the vanilla essence, followed by the milk. Finally, beat in the melted chocolate until a good spreading consistency is achieved.

7 To decorate yule log, remove paper and cover and fill with buttercream. Mark on lines with a fork to resemble wood, sprinkle with icing sugar, and decorate with holly or Christmas novelties.

CLOCKWISE FROM BOTTOM:
Chocolate Yule Log,
Twelfth Night Cake,
Boiled Fruit Cake variation (see page 8),
decorated with sugarpaste (rolled
fondant icing) and flowers.

Fruity fayre

Fruity, continental yuletide treats make wonderful additions to any Christmas feast. Italian Panettone is a nice light alternative to all the rich foods of the festive season. While German Stollen fruit bread makes a good gift for friends, wrapped in red ribbons to contrast with the white sugar.

stollen

1 To make the yeast batter, blend the fresh yeast into the milk. Mix in the flour and leave in a warm place until frothy (this should take about 20 minutes).

2 Sift the flour and salt into a bowl and stir in the sugar, then rub in the butter until it resembles fine crumbs. Make a well in the middle, add the egg and the yeast batter and mix to a soft dough. Turn on to a floured surface and knead until smooth. Return to the bowl, cover with cling film and leave to rise until doubled in size (about 1 hour).

3 Grease a baking sheet. Place the dough on the floured surface and knead lightly to knock out the air. Press the almonds, zest, currants, sultanas and peel into the dough and knead until well mixed in.

4 Roll out the dough to a round 25 cm (10 in) in diameter. Brush the surface with the melted butter, then spread the cherries in a strip across the centre. Fold the dough over into three to cover the cherries. Place on the baking sheet, brush with melted butter and cover with cling film again. Leave to prove until light and puffy (about 30 minutes).

5 Preheat the oven to 200ºC (400ºF/gas mark 6). Bake towards the top of the oven for about 35 minutes, until golden, then cool on a wire rack. Dredge heavily with icing sugar when cold. Serve sliced and buttered.

panettone

1 Grease an 18 cm (7 in) round deep cake tin and line with a double band of greased greaseproof paper to come 10 cm (4 in) higher than the rim of the tin. Secure the join with a paper clip.

2 Sift the flour and nutmeg into a large bowl and make a well in the centre. Blend the yeast with the milk until dissolved, then pour into the flour. Gradually draw in the flour from the sides and mix together well to make a soft dough. Cover the bowl with a clean cloth and leave to rise in a warm place until the dough is doubled in size (about 1 hour).

3 Turn out the dough onto a floured surface. Knead to knock out the air, until the dough is smooth, then gradually mix in the butter in pieces, followed by the egg yolks. Gently mix in the sugar, peel, sultanas and zest until well combined.

4 Cover with a cloth and leave to rise for 45 minutes or until doubled in size. Place the dough in the tin, and leave to rise again until it reaches halfway up the paper lining.

5 Preheat the oven to 200ºC (400ºF/gas mark 6). Cut a cross right through the dough. Brush the surface with beaten egg yolk or milk and bake for 20 minutes, then turn down the oven temperature to 180ºC (350ºF/gas mark 4) and bake for a further 30-40 minutes or until a skewer inserted into the centre comes out clean.

6 Leave the cake to cool in the tin for 10 minutes, then turn out on to a wire rack to cool completely. Dust with sifted icing sugar when cold. Eat within 5 days.

OPPOSITE: Stollen.

Traditional treats

Biscuits and shortbread make excellent presents, in fact Scottish shortbread is traditionally given to welcome in the New Year. Spiced Lebkuchen make very good tree decorations as well as being delicious treats. Traditionally heart-shaped, they look and taste just as good whatever shape you make them. Thread them with ribbon and hang from the tree.

YOU WILL NEED

275 g (10 oz) plain flour
50 g (2 oz) rice flour
pinch of salt
75 g (3 oz) caster sugar
250 g (9 oz) butter
caster sugar, to decorate
MAKES **16** WEDGES

Scottish shortbread

1 Preheat the oven to to 160ºC (325ºF/gas mark 3). Grease two baking sheets.

2 Sift flours and salt into a bowl and stir in the caster sugar. Add the butter, cut into small pieces, and rub into the dry ingredients until the mixture resembles crumbs. You will then find that it can be kneaded into a soft dough, using no liquid.

3 Knead until a smooth ball is formed. Cut it in half and roll out each piece into a 20 cm (8 in) round. Mark into eight wedges, and flute the edges like pastry, then prick with a fork.

4 Place a round on each baking sheet. Bake in preheated oven for 30-40 minutes or until pale golden. Leave to cool completely on the sheets, as the warm shortbread is very soft to handle.

5 Dust with caster sugar, and tie up with red ribbons.

lebkuchen

1 Preheat the oven to to 180°C (350°F/gas mark 4). Melt the honey and the brown sugar in a pan. Bring to the boil and then remove from the heat. Add the spices, brandy, butter, bicarbonate of soda and baking powder and stir until the butter has melted and the mixture is clear and smooth.

2 Sift the flour into a bowl and pour in the honey mixture, folding it in to form a soft dough.

3 Roll the dough out on a floured surface to a thickness of 6 mm (¼ in). Cut out using pastry cutters of your own choice.

4 Make a hole at the top of each biscuit through which to thread a ribbon. Bake on a buttered baking sheet in the preheated oven for 10 minutes until the biscuits are golden brown. When cool, add a little white icing, if you wish.

<table>
<tr><td>

YOU WILL NEED

40 g (1½ oz) dark runny honey

40 g (1½ oz) soft dark brown sugar

pinch of fresh ground nutmeg

pinch of cinnamon

pinch of ginger

pinch of cloves

1 tsp brandy

50 g (2 oz) butter

pinch of bicarbonate of soda

pinch of baking powder

100 g (4 oz) plain flour

icing sugar (optional)

narrow ribbon, to hang

MAKES **8-10** BISCUITS

</td></tr>
</table>

Christmas cracker cake

This novel way of decorating an ordinary square fruit cake should tempt even the most turkey-stuffed palate on Christmas afternoon. You could decorate the board with small gifts appropriate to your guests or arrange real crackers around them to make a stunning centrepiece for the Christmas table.

YOU WILL NEED

INGREDIENTS

20 cm (8 in) square fruit cake
(see page 9)

4 tbsp brandy

3 tbsp apricot jam

1 kg (2 lb 4 oz) marzipan

black, red and green food
colour pastes

950 g (33 oz) sugarpaste
(rolled fondant icing), divided
and coloured as follows:
150 g (5 oz) black
400 g (14 oz) red
400 g (14 oz) green

1 tbsp white royal icing
(see page 24)

icing sugar, for rolling out

UTENSILS

30 cm (12 in) gold-coloured
square cake board

carving knife

small sharp knife

cocktail stick (toothpick)

pastry brush

rolling pin

cake smoothers

clingfilm (plastic wrap)

paintbrush

No 3 piping nozzle (round tip)

piping (decorating) bag fitted
with No 1 nozzle (round tip)

2 m (2 yards 7 in) tartan ribbon

fish slice (pancake turner)

1 Cut the cake into two 7.5 cm (3 in) strips. Use the remaining cake to extend the length of the first two strips (fig 1). Run a knife along the two long edges of each cracker to slightly round them.

2 Pierce both cakes a few times using a cocktail stick and pour the brandy over the holes.

3 Cover both crackers with a pastry brush dipped into warmed apricot jam.

4 Dust your work surface with a little icing sugar and knead 500 g (1 lb 2 oz) marzipan until pliable. Smooth down the marzipan over one cake using your hands and a pair of cake smoothers and trim away any excess. Press a finger round the cracker to make a dent about 5 cm (2 in) from one end. Repeat at the other end. (This 'dent' is visible in fig 2.)

5 Repeat step 4 on the second cracker.

6 Measure the ends of the crackers and moisten with a little water. Roll out the black sugarpaste (rolled fondant icing). Cut out four circles slightly larger than the ends of the crackers. Stick one circle onto each end.

7 Moisten the ends of the cracker with water. Roll out 200 g (7 oz) red sugarpaste and cut out two strips about 20 x 7.5 cm (8 x 3 in) Serrate one edge and wind around one end of the cracker (fig 2). Press the back of a knife into the icing a few times to make creases and tweak the jagged edges so that they stand out slightly. If they keep flopping, support them with a ball of scrunched up clingfilm (plastic wrap) until they dry.

8 Roll out 200 g (7 oz) of green sugarpaste. Cut out a strip 20 x 18 cm (8 x 7 in). Moisten the centre of the cracker and wind the strip around it. Take a No 3 piping nozzle and press a line of decorative circles along both edges of the strip.

1

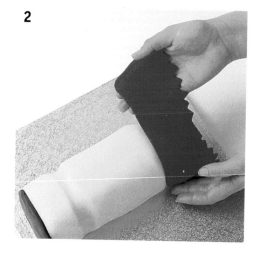

2

9 Repeat the above procedures on the second cracker, except this time use green sugarpaste for the ends of the cracker and red for the central strip.

3

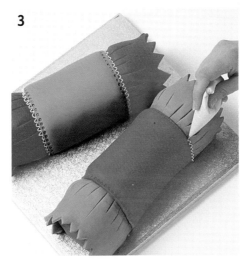

10 Pipe small loops along the edges of the central strips using a No 1 nozzle and white royal icing (fig 3).

11 Pipe a line of small dots around the jagged edges of both crackers.

12 Lift and arrange both crackers on the hoard using a fish slice (pancake turner).

13 Cut two strips of tartan ribbon approximately 26 cm (10 in) long. Place one diagonally across the central strip of each cracker and secure with a little royal icing.

14 Finally, make two neat bows and stick on the top of each cracker with a little blob of royal icing.

Christmas stocking cake

Just when everyone thinks that they've had all their surprises for the day, present this cake and wait for the gasps of admiration. If you have the time (usually in very short supply just before Christmas!) you could make small icing models for all the family and substitute them for the presents.

YOU WILL NEED

INGREDIENTS

20 cm (8 in) square fruit cake
(see page 9)

3 tbsp brandy

3 tbsp apricot jam

775 g (1 lb 12 oz) marzipan

red and green food colour pastes

1 kg 675 g (3 lb 12 oz)
sugarpaste (rolled fondant
icing), divided and coloured
as follows:
900 g (2 lb) red
275 g (10 oz) green
500 g (1 lb 2 oz) left white

26 edible gold balls

1 tsp red royal icing
(see page 24)

icing sugar, for rolling out

UTENSILS

30 cm (12 in) gold-coloured
square cake board

carving knife

small sharp knife

cocktail stick (toothpick)

pastry brush

rolling pin

cake smoothers

small holly cutter

icing nozzle (tip)

piping (decorating) bag fitted
with No 1 nozzle (round tip)

small plastic bags, for
storing icing

1 Cut the cake in two so that one section measures 11.5 x 20 cm (4½ x 8 in) and the other 8.5 x 20 cm (3½ x 8 in). Place the thinner of the two strips at the base of the thicker one to produce the basic stocking shape (fig 1). Cut small triangles away from the toe and heel of the stocking and also run a knife along the edges of the cake to make them rounded. Cut a slice about 2.5 cm (1 in) off the top of the cake to make the proportions look right and discard this piece.

2 Pierce the cake several times with a cocktail stick (toothpick) and drizzle the brandy over the cake. Allow the brandy to sink in, then place the cake onto the cake board.

3 Using a pastry brush, 'paint' the cake with warmed apricot jam.

4 Knead the marzipan on a surface dusted with icing sugar until it's nice and pliable. Roll it out into a rectangle approximately 6 mm (¼ in) thick and lift it over the cake. Ease it gently into position and trim away any excess marzipan. Run over the surface with cake smoothers.

5 Moisten the marzipan with a little water.

6 Knead and roll out 700 g (1 lb 8 oz) of the red sugarpaste (rolled fondant icing). Lay this carefully over the marzipan. Trim away the excess and keep this for modelling the presents later. Neaten the top and sides of the stocking with cake smoothers.

7 For the presents, you will need 200 g (7 oz) of red sugarpaste, 220 g (8 oz) of green sugarpaste and 100 g (4 oz) of white (fig 2). Make two 50 g (2 oz) red squares for presents, a green and white ball, using about 50 g (2 oz) of both green and white. Then make a completely green 50 g (2 oz) ball.

For the candy canes, roll out two 25 g (1 oz) sausages (ropes) of contrasting coloured icing. Twist the two sausages together and bend into a walking stick shape. Make three. Keep two back and pile the other one and the presents and balls up against the top of stocking, securing them with a little water.

8 Knead and roll 400 g (14 oz) white sugarpaste into a strip about 28 cm (11 in) long and about 15 cm (6 in) wide. Moisten the top of the stocking

and lay the cuff into position so that it overlaps the presents slightly. Hold a piping nozzle (tip) at a slight angle and press it into the white to leave impressions in the still soft icing.

9 Slot the last two candy canes into position and secure with water.

10 Stick small flattened balls of white sugarpaste onto one of the red parcels to decorate it.

11 Thinly roll out 50 g (2 oz) green icing and cut out 26 holly leaves with a cutter. Stick these onto the cake in pairs and press the back of a knife into each one three times to make veins (fig 3).

12 Attach two gold balls beneath each pair of leaves using the red royal icing in the piping (decorating) bag and two tiny balls of red icing beneath the leaves on the cuff.

3

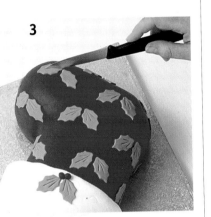

Tip

To take a lot of the hard work out of kneading marzipan, heat it in a microwave for a few seconds. However, don't overdo it or the oil in the centre will get very hot and could give you a nasty burn.

Christmas Santas cake

Ideal for anyone who loves the nuts and marzipan that abound around Christmas-time, this is an extremely easy cake to decorate. Try to use white marzipan rather than yellow as this takes the colours better.

YOU WILL NEED

INGREDIENTS

20 cm (8 in) round fruit cake (see step 1 before baking.)

selection of nuts, such as almonds, pecans, hazelnut, walnuts, etc.

3 tbsp brandy (optional)

4 tbsp apricot jam

icing sugar, for rolling out

red, paprika, dark brown and green food colour pastes

720 g (1 lb 9¼ oz) white (neutral) marzipan, divided and coloured as follows:
240 g (8¼ oz) red
150 g (5 oz) flesh colour (paprika)
120 g (4 oz) dark brown
30 g (1 oz) green
leave the remaining marzipan white (neutral)

UTENSILS

greaseproof paper

23 cm (9 in) round cake board

cocktail stick

sieve

pastry brush

rolling pin

small sharp knife

water and paintbrush

1

1 Follow the boiled fruit cake recipe for a 20 cm (8 in) round cake on page 8 to the point where you have spooned the mixture into the baking tin. Before placing it in the oven, arrange a selection of nuts over the top of the mixture. Use your favourite nuts or whatever you have in your store-cupboard and start from the outside of the cake and work in. I began with a circle of almonds, then a line of pecans. Next came a circle of hazelnuts, some nice big chunky brazil nuts and finally half a walnut in the centre.

Trim a piece of greaseproof paper to fit over the top of the tin and cut a small hole about 3 cm (1¼ in) out of the centre. Rest this over the cake before baking to stop the nuts browning too much during the cooking process. If you have a fan oven, use a sheet of greaseproof paper long enough to tuck under the baking tin, otherwise it will simply fly off as soon as you shut the door.

Bake as normal, removing the greaseproof paper about 10 minutes before the end of the cooking time just to lightly brown and colour the nuts.

2 When the cake has cooled, turn it out of the tin and place onto a 23 cm (9 in) round cake board.

For an extra festive touch, pierce the cake a few times between the nuts with a cocktail stick (you

can lift a few up if you wish) and carefully drizzle about 2 tbsp of brandy over the cake. Allow it to seep in and replace any nuts you might have moved.

Boil the apricot jam either in a saucepan or in a non-metallic dish in a microwave for about one minute. Sieve the jam to remove any lumps of fruit and mix in the last remaining tablespoon of brandy. (You may omit the brandy if you prefer.) Paint the mixture over the top and sides of the cake using a pastry brush to give it a wonderfully gleaming finish (fig 1).

3 To make the 12 figures, begin with the bodies. Sprinkle your worksurface with icing sugar. Take a 15 g (½ oz) piece of red-coloured marzipan and roll it into a flattish conical shape. Press and stick the body up against the side of the cake. You shouldn't need any water to keep it in place – the jam around the sides should be adequate to hold it.

Make another identical body and stick this directly opposite. Stick the third and fourth bodies halfway between the first two (fig 2). The cake should now be divided into quarters. Make and stick another two bodies between each of the four Santas already in position, leaving a small space between each one for his sack. Continue until all the bodies are evenly spaced around the side of the cake.

2

4 To make a head, roll a 10 g (¼ oz) ball of flesh-coloured marzipan into an oval shape (fig 3). Stick this on top of one of the bodies already in position. Repeat on the other eleven Santas.

5 For each hat, form 5 g (⅛ oz) of red marzipan into a small triangular shape. Tweak the end into a point and bend it over slightly. Place it on one of the heads. The tip of the hat should rest just on top of the cake. Repeat and make hats for all the other figures, ensuring that they all point in the same direction.

6 To make the beards, thinly roll out 10 g (¼ oz) of white (neutral) marzipan. Press lines into the marzipan using the back of a knife and cut out a triangular shape. Stick this onto Santa's face so that the beard hangs over the front of the body. If it won't stay in place, use a little water.

Push the end of a paintbrush into the beard to leave behind a surprised, open-mouthed expression. Stick on a tiny ball of flesh-coloured marzipan for Santa's nose. Repeat on each Santa.

7 To decorate a hat, take about 5 g (⅛ oz) of white marzipan. Pull off a tiny piece and roll it into a ball for the pom-pom. Stick in place. Roll the rest into a sausage and lay it around the brim of the hat so that it almost obscures all the face. Repeat on the rest of the hats.

8 Use 10 g (¼ oz) brown marzipan for each sack and shape into a cone. Stand each one on its fattest part, then pinch and pull the marzipan at the top to make a neck (fig 3). Press one between each Santa on the side of the cake.

9 To make the presents, roll out 30 g (1 oz) green marzipan to a thickness of about 1 cm (⅜ in). Cut out twelve tiny green squares. Using the back of a knife, make a criss-cross pattern on the front of each parcel. Place one in the top of each sack and bend the neck of the sack up slightly. Brush away any dusty icing sugar marks using a damp paintbrush.

3

Christmas reindeer cake

YOU WILL NEED

1 Moist Christmas Cake
(see page 9)
marzipan, to cover cake

ICING
1 egg white
560 g (1 lb 2 oz) icing sugar
1 tsp lemon juice

DECORATIONS
white marzipan, for modelling
green, red, paprika, and brown
food colourings
icing sugar, for dusting
egg white
brown food colouring pen

UTENSILS
23 cm (9 in) square cake board
side scraper paper
palette knife
scissors
small sharp knife
modelling tool

It is always fun at Christmas to have novelty figures on a cake rather than shop-bought items. The hand-modelled Father Christmas, sack, presents, trees and reindeer are made from marzipan. The cake is a 20 cm (8 in) square moist fruit cake covered in marzipan (see page 9), with a flat top and peaked royal icing sides. Arrange the figures on top of the cake and to finish, trim the board with ribbon.

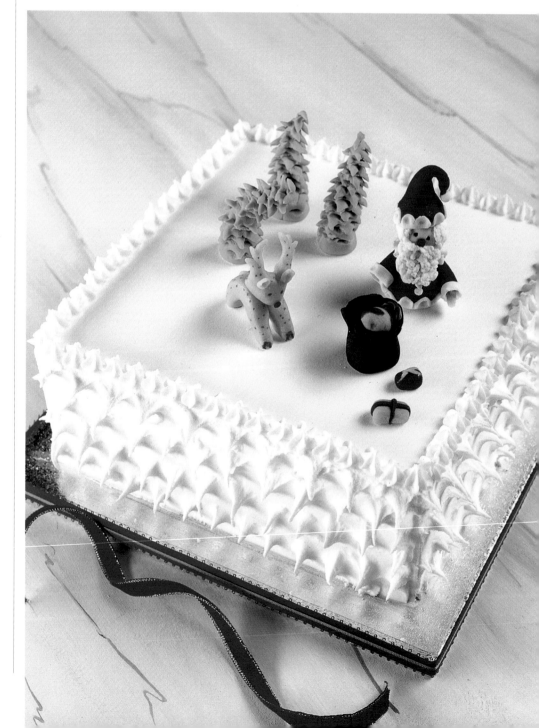

1 To make the royal icing, beat egg white until foamy. Gradually beat in icing sugar, beating well after each addition.

2 When mixture reaches soft peak stage, beat in lemon juice. Continue to add icing sugar and beat until stiff.

to make royal icing peaks
Spread one side of the cake with royal icing, and smooth the icing with a side scraper to give a fairly even surface.

Press the palette knife dipped in royal icing on the side of the cake. Pull away sharply to form a peak. Repeat to form staggered rows of peaks along the side of the cake. If the icing becomes too messy just smooth it off and start the process again.

to make the decorations
Break down the marzipan into the number of pieces you require and colour them accordingly, keading them well until evenly coloured and smooth. Dust the work surface with icing sugar. Christmas trees: mould pieces of green marzipan into cone shapes and, using a pair of scissors, snip into the marzipan from the point of the cone, working around the cone to the base.

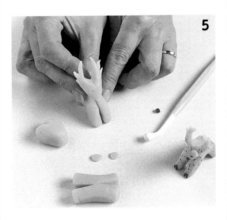

father Christmas:
Cut out and shape from red marzipan a body, a hat, two sleeves and a red nose. Cut out and shape from white marzipan the edging to go around the base of the body, the hat and the sleeves. Cut out the beard shape and cover with white marzipan pressed through a sieve; also use this for his hair. Colour some flesh tone marzipan using paprika colouring and shape the head and hands. Assemble the parts using egg white to secure. Mark the eyes with the brown food colouring pen.

reindeer:
Using brown-coloured marzipan, shape an oblong body piece and make a cut at each end to within 1 cm (½ in) of the centre. Shape the hoofs and bend to form front and back legs. Mould a heart-shaped piece for the head, press the top curves into antlers and snip with a pair of scissors to shape. Place in position on the body, attach the ears and make a red nose. Use the brown food colouring pen for the markings.

sack with presents:
Shape a piece of brown marzipan into a ball. Using a modelling tool, press the inside to make it hollow, making the edge thinner. Shape presents from red and green marzipan.

Winter warmers

peel of a lemon
6 whole cloves
ground cinnamon to taste
pinch of grated nutmeg
5 parts red Bordeaux-style wine
1 part ruby port
1 part brandy

What could be better than a warming tipple on a chilly winter's evening? Popular over the festive season, these traditional drinks are ideal to offer all the friends and relatives that pop by at this time of year.

mulled claret

Mulled wine has been a traditional winter drink for centuries. Modern recipes, compared with those of days gone by, are slightly more refined, better tasting and certainly with more of a kick.

1 Place the lemon peel, cloves, cinnamon and nutmeg in a saucepan, add the liquid ingredients and heat slowly until almost, but not quite, boiling. If it is allowed to boil it loses its alcohol.

2 Strain the drink into a warmed coffee mug.

Mulled Claret was originally made simply by heating a fire poker and plunging it into a tankard of wine.

peel of a lemon or orange
whole cloves
1 tbsp brown sugar
1 cinnamon stick
a liberal helping of dark Jamaican rum
half as much crème de cacao
a pat of unsalted butter
grated nutmeg

hot buttered rum

This is a warm, sustaining drink to serve on a freezing winter's night by a roaring log fire. Buttered rum is mentioned by Charles Dickens in his book, *Hard Times*. "Take a glass of scalding rum and butter before you get into bed," Bounderby says to Mrs Sparsit.

1 Warm a large coffee mug by filling it with boiling water and letting it stand for a minute. While it is warming, take the citrus peel and stud it with as many whole cloves as you can.

2 Empty the coffee mug and place the studded peel in it, together with the brown sugar and cinnamon stick. Add a little boiling water and stir until the sugar has dissolved.

3 Now add the rum and crème de cacao and fill the mug with hot water.

4 Remove the cinnamon stick. Drop in the butter, stir and sprinkle with grated nutmeg.

YOU WILL NEED

crushed ice

2 sherry glasses of amontillado sherry

1 dessertspoon caster sugar (or to taste)

1 fresh egg

1 cup of milk

grated nutmeg

sherry eggnog

The Sherry Eggnog is a smooth and sensual drink with a velvety texture.

1 Place half a cup of crushed ice in a blender or cocktail shaker. Add the sherry, caster sugar, egg and milk and shake or blend until smooth and velvety.

2 Strain into a chilled highball glass and dust with grated nutmeg.

Quite apart from being a delicious, silky-smooth drink, the Sherry Eggnog is reputed to be soothing for a sore throat and helpful for a hangover.

1 part Irish whisky

5 parts strong, black coffee

1 tsp brown sugar

1 part thick cream

Irish coffee

This is a fine alternative to ordinary coffee at the end of a festive meal. You can actually buy an Irish liqueur called Irish Velvet, which is based on Irish whisky, black coffee and sugar. It's not as pleasant, or as much fun, as making your own.

1 Pour the Irish whisky and hot coffee into a warmed Irish coffee glass, which is sometimes a goblet with a handle like a teacup and sometimes shaped like a large wineglass.

2 Add brown sugar to taste and stir gently until it is dissolved.

3 Trickle the cream over the back of a teaspoon onto the surface of the coffee.

1 cube of sugar

dash of Angostura bitters

chilled dry champagne

1 tsp brandy

1 cocktail cherry

champagne classic

There are several versions of the Champagne Classic, some of which leave out the brandy. It's a simple and deliciously elegant drink for the Christmas season.

1 Place the cube of sugar in a champagne flute and add a dash or two of Angostura bitters.

2 Carefully fill the glass with champagne.

3 Add the teaspoon of brandy.

4 Serve decorated with the cocktail cherry.

Christmas Decorations

Christmas is a time of year when no home goes without a little extra decoration to add to the festive atmosphere. Fresh and artificial fruits, flowers and foliage, made up into garlands and wreaths or adorning gift boxes, convey a sense of natural bounty. Indulge your senses with the spicy aromas of scented pomanders or the fresh fragrance of pine cones.

Winter garland

Parchment flowers are perfect for winter garlands. They do not fade or wither, and look really elegant in almost any setting. These creamy, green peony roses are set on a white painted vine wreath against fake cotoneaster foliage and teamed with gilded paper figs and dried orange slices. It's a pleasure to have this garland hanging at any time of year, but it makes an unusual and refreshing change at Christmas.

1

If you can only buy a natural vine wreath, paint it white first with emulsion paint. Once dry, rub the wreath with a piece of sandpaper to distress the surface and reveal some of the natural wood that is beneath.

2

Using secateurs or scissors, cut the foliage into manageable pieces and twist them in and out of the wreath, working in one direction only, until the base is virtually covered. Make sure that you reveal some of the white wreath base though. Use lengths of the reel wire to keep the foliage in place.

3

Trim down the peony roses using secateurs or wire cutters and push the stems into the wreath. Keep the flowers at an equal distance apart, and peel open their petals once they are in position. (Parchment flowers are packaged with the petals and leaves tucked in. It's easy to mould and tweak these into shape: they are much more manageable and obedient than their fresh cousins!)

4

Put a little gold paint on your finger and rub on to the fake figs to add highlights. Cut down their stems with wire cutters or secateurs and slot into the display. I have only used two bunches to add a change of texture and interest to the garland.

5

Finally, plug in the hot glue gun and once the glue has melted, stick the dried orange slices and small dried oranges in place around the wreath. Hot glue sticks rapidly, so work quickly. If you make a mistake, pull the piece off immediately, as items can be quite difficult to remove once the glue has dried. Create a hanging loop at the back of the garland with the stub wire.

Variations

For a more traditional garland, use fake fir or pine foliage with gilded cones, clusters of artificial berries and bright red, silk poinsettias.

Swedish Candelabra

Simple but attractive decoration can be added to an existing candelabra to give it a more festive air. With a very simple twiggy wreath, you could add small silver or gold decorations, such as silver-sprayed tiny fruit (kumquats are ideal), small cones wired to the base, plastic berries in silver or gold, added in small bunches, and silver or gold candles. Match the candle colours to those of the decoration. Take care to ensure that none of the leaves or branches actually touch the candles themselves. In any event, no lit candles should be left unattended.

YOU WILL NEED

several branches of birch

florist's reel wire

scissors

candelabra

several branches of rosehips

candles to fit

1 Take three birch branches and bind the stems together at the base with reel wire.

2 Loosely bind the wire up towards the tip of the branches to pull together any wayward stems. Do not pull the wire so tight that the sideshoots are all uniformly tucked in. Small shoots should stray out at either side.

3 Take the next three stems and add them to the first three about two thirds of the way along, base to tip, wrapping them loosely with reel wire as you do so.

4 Bind the tips of the stems to the base of the first stems to make a rough circle to fit the diameter of your candelabra. Bind together to complete the circle.

5 Add the circle of twiggy branches to the base of the candelabra, wiring it on securely at each candleholder.

6 Add the rosehips, pushing the thicker ends of the branches into the twiggy base.

Variation

This version (right) shows the same cast iron candelabra, but decorated this time with alder twigs, complete with small greenish-brown cones. Green candles complete the display, toning with the colours of the foliage and the cones.

Festive twig tree

YOU WILL NEED

knife

dry oasis

terracotta pot

4-5 twiggy branches – about 38 cm (15 in) tall

pea gravel

kumquats and cloves for the pomanders

medium-gauge wire

secateurs

tartan bows

fruit rings

gold-sprayed cones, baskets and seedheads

metallic baubles

artificial birds

This sparkly twig tree is ideal as a simple, quick decorating idea. If you put the tree in or near the window, the gold- or silver-sprayed decorations will catch the light beautifully. Choose highly branched twigs and anchor them in a stable base. Florist's dry oasis works very well, but make sure the pot is deep enough to take a reasonably large block. Some of the decorations for this tree, such as the artificial birds, are shop-bought from a hobby store; others are homemade. If you wish, you can make small wreaths to hang on the tree (see page 39). You can make these from whatever small fruits and berries you can find.

1 Cut the oasis into a wedge shaped block to fit snugly inside the container.

2 Arrange the four or five twigs so that they fan out attractively.

3 Fill the container with pea gravel so that the oasis is covered. Finally hang the branches with the decorations of your choice (see overleaf).

Kumquat pomanders

Kumquats – small citrus fruit the colour of oranges – are ideal for making pomanders for a festive twig tree. You can buy them from the supermarket during the winter and stud them with dried cloves in whatever patterns you find most attractive.

1 Assemble the fruit and the cloves with which to stud them on a work surface. It is quite a messy business so use a wipeable top on which to work, or spread paper on the surface.

2 Insert the cloves in lines around the fruit, gently pushing the pointed end of the clove into the fruit. You can create a circle of cloves around the diameter of the fruit, or make a quartered pattern. Alternatively, stud the whole fruit with cloves.

3 Wire each fruit using medium-gauge florist's wire. Push a length of wire right through the fruit and back again and twist to secure, creating a hook as you do so.

4 Hang the fruits on the twig tree, or, if you wish, use them as decorations for a Christmas tree or garland.

YOU WILL NEED

kumquats
cloves
medium-gauge florist's wire

Mini decorations

You can make all sorts of small decorations from different kinds of fruits and cones, either as mini wreaths or simply by spraying the fruit or nuts with gold or silver spray paint.

miniature berry wreaths

Pyracantha berries can be wired in bunches onto a mini wreath, and a narrow ribbon used to hang it from the tree.

sprayed decorations

Various dried or artificial small decorations can be sprayed with gold paint, such as seedheads, a little basket filled with tiny fruits or flowers or a pine cone. Hang them on the tree with narrow gold ribbons.

miniature dried fruit wreaths

Dried cranberries or raisins can be strung onto a short length of florist's wire, twisted at the ends to form a ring, and decorated with a simple bow.

Scented pine cones

Pine cones, piled high in a wooden bowl, become an eye-catching aromatic feature when their fragrance is enhanced with essential oils. A wonderful gift can be created by lining a box with felt and filling it with the scented pine cones. The felt will absorb the fragrance and provide a colourful backdrop to the cones.

1 Place the cones in the mixing bowl. Add the pine or cedarwood oil to the pine cones, turning the cones as you do so to ensure that the oil is well dispersed.

2 Cover the mixing bowl tightly with cling film and leave to stand for 1 week to allow the oils to penetrate the cones.

3 Place the cones in a decorative container. The oil will slowly evaporate into the room, scenting the air as it does so. Once the scent has faded the cones can be revived by repeating the process above. If you have an open fire, you can throw a cone or two in occasionally for an intense burst of fragrance.

Orange & clove pomanders

Studded all over with spicy cloves, these orange pomanders are packed into festive coloured tissue paper and a pretty box. They will stay richly fragrant for months. You could also wrap them in muslin and two or three layers of gold and silver net, tie with a ribbon and bells and hang them on your Christmas tree to scent the room and to be given to guests as they depart.

1 Mix all the spices and the orris root in a bowl.

2 Pierce a line of holes around half an orange and stud with cloves. Repeat this process until the whole orange is covered. Keep them fairly close together, but leave sufficient room to allow for shrinkage.

3 Place the orange in the bowl of spices, tossing gently so that the whole surface has come into contact with the spices. Repeat this process for the other oranges. Cover the bowl tightly with cling film.

4 Turn the pomanders daily (or as often as you remember) for one month. They will then be ready to remove from the spices and use.

Christmas box

YOU WILL NEED

oval, Shaker-style box

paintbrushes (optional)

acrylic paints (optional)

dry oasis

PVA glue

cuttings of evergreens such as
holly and ivy

small pine cones with stems
attached

wide satin ribbon

This wonderful seasonal box is very simple to make, yet beautifully effective. It is decorated with sprigs of evergreen foliage fixed to a square of florist's dry foam on the lid. A ribbon bow completes the design. It's a fantastic way to present your gifts.

1 If necessary, paint the box in a colour to suit. Leave to dry, then glue a block of dry oasis to the lid using PVA glue. Insert branches of holly and evergreen into the foam. Start by working around the perimeter of the foam with the larger cuttings, and then build up the design by filling in the gaps with smaller pieces and pine cones.

2 When you have achieved a pleasing result, tie a wide ribbon around the box, and finish with a large bow. Adjust the bow so that it sits well on the greenery.

Variation

This box (right) has been covered in ochre paper and embellished with bands of metallic ribbon and gold and red tinsel. Red baubles and glittery apples are heaped onto the lid, and stuck in place with a strong adhesive.

Christmas Cards

Shop-bought Christmas cards are both expensive and much less personal than handmade cards. Surprise your loved ones with an individual greeting this year and see the difference it makes! Many of the designs can be adapted to make attractive gift tags or can be easily and quickly mass produced – make one for all your friends and family. Choose a stencil project, such as the Robin Red Breast design on page 48, and you could even make matching gift wrap.

Christmas window

YOU WILL NEED

acetate photocopies of image
pencil and metal ruler
set square
craft knife
cutting board
A5 sheet of white card
silver glitter glue
scissors
double-sided tape
A5 sheet of white paper
glue stick

Photocopying onto acetate can create really beautiful images, perfect for card-making. Take photographs of leaves against a background of sky or lay them on a sheet of plain white card. Images with a light background and a strong central subject work best. Here holly leaves make a sophisticated, seasonal card.

BELOW:
The holly and the ivy;
seasonal gift tags made using
the same technique.

The image area needs to be 7.5 x 7.5 cm
(3 x 3 in). Choose the best photocopied
image and trim it to size.

Cut a piece of white card 10 x 21 cm
(4 x 8½ in). Score and fold in half. This is
the card blank.

To create the central window, mark a 2 cm
(¾ in) border all around the front of the card
and carefully cut out the central square
using a craft knife.

Spread a little silver glitter glue around the
border on the front of the card. Leave to dry.

Attach the acetate to the back of the
window using double-sided adhesive tape.

Cut a piece of white paper into a rectangle
9.5 x 20 cm (3¾ x 8 in) and fold in half.
Apply a small line of glue down the inside
spine of the card and stick the inner leaf
in position.

Robin red breast

YOU WILL NEED

pencil and metal ruler
tracing paper
glue stick
thin card
craft knife
cutting board
gold acrylic paint
saucer
sponge
black tissue paper
red glitter glue
black felt tip pen
A5 sheet of cream textured card
scissors
gold foil
A5 sheet of red textured paper

Stencilling is an excellent technique to use when you need to make lots of cards. Commercially produced stencils are available from art and craft shops, but they are also fairly simple to make yourself and once you have the stencil, prints are quick to make.

Draw a robin shape on a piece of plain paper. Use the glue stick to attach it to the thin card. Cut out the shape carefully with a craft knife. It is a good idea to prepare two or three stencils, especially if you want to make a lot of cards.

Pour a little gold paint onto a saucer and press the sponge into the paint. Do not use too much paint. Spread the black tissue paper out, hold the stencil firmly in place and dab the sponge onto the stencil. You might want to stencil more robins than you will need and use the best prints.

Once the gold paint is dry, dab the red glitter glue onto the robin's breast. Make a black dot for its eye with the felt tip pen. Now you are ready to put the card together.

Make a card base by folding the cream card in half. As this card has a naive feel to it, the layers are cut approximately to shape. The first layer is a rectangle of gold foil approximately 7.5 x 9.5 cm (3 x 3¾ in), glued onto the cream card. Glue in a high central position on the card base.

The second layer is a rectangle approximately 6.5 x 7.5 cm (2¾ x 3 in) cut from red textured paper. Glue it on top of the gold. Finally, cut out a rectangle around the robin motif, approximately 5 x 6 cm (2 x 2½ in) and glue it on top of the red paper.

ABOVE:
Put your stencil to good use and make an interesting selection of cards.

Frost at Christmas time

This ice-cold winter scene is created from a collage of silver foils and textured white papers, and arranged as a simple three-fold card. Glitter paint and glinting silver sequin stars add to the wintry atmosphere.

1 Cut a rectangle 51 x 15 cm (20 x 6 in) from thin white card. Score two fold lines at 17 cm (6½ in) intervals along the longest edge, to make a three-fold card.

2 On the centre panel, mark a border 1 cm (⅜ in) in from the outside edge - but do not cut out.

3 Within this border, using the templates below as a guide, draw peaks across the top half of the card, to form a mountain range and draw a second zigzag line across the lower quarter of the card to form a jagged ice effect.

4 Fold the card front (centre rectangle) and fold-in flap card sections together. The, cutting through both card thicknesses, cut out these marked areas to make cut-out 'sky' and 'water' sections.

5 Cut a rectangle about 14.5 x 5.5 cm (5¾ x 2¼ in) from both the white textured tissue paper and one of the silver papers.

6 Stick these paper rectangles to the inside of the card, so that the tissue paper covers the cut-out above the mountain range, and the silver paper creates the freezing water along the jagged ice edge.

7 Stick the fold-in flap in place over the back of the card front with stick adhesive.

8 Cut some small pine tree shapes from the second silver paper. Stick these in place as desired on the front of the card.

9 Use some silver glitter paint to decorate the mountain peaks with a scattering of "snow". Apply this lightly for a subtle effect.

10 Finish off the card by sticking a few sequin stars to the tissue paper "sky" above the mountain peaks.

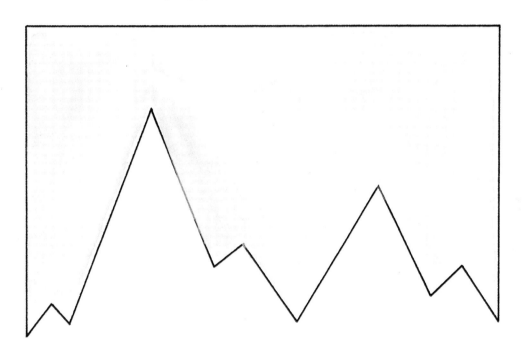

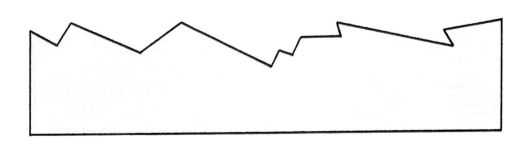

Host of angels

YOU WILL NEED

pencil

scrap paper

scissors

A4 sheet of white cartridge paper

gold marker pen

A4 sheet of gold paper

glue stick

These stylish cut-and-fold paper angels will look great on the mantelpiece at Christmas. Paper-cutting is always a favourite with children, so get them involved and see what they come up with. Once you have made the template this card is quick and easy to make, so start a production line and make them for all your friends.

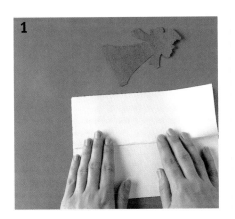

1

Using a pencil and scrap paper draw an angel shape, using the photograph as a guide. It should be roughly 18 cm (6 in) deep and 7.5 cm (2⅞ in) wide. Cut around the shape to make the template. Fold a sheet of white A4 cartridge paper in half, then open flat. Now fold from each side in towards the centre and run your finger along the folds to flatten them. Re-fold the centre to create a zigzag fold with four sections.

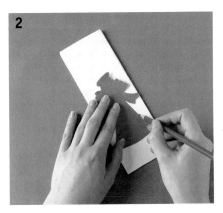

2

Place the angel template on the front of the folded sheet. Use the pencil to draw around the shape.

3

Cut out the angel, making sure you do not trim the folds where the hands and the bottom of the skirts meet – these points hold the design together. Open out.

4

To decorate the angels, use the gold pen to draw an outline and to add the details, following the photograph opposite.

5

Fold the gold paper into a four-section zigzag (as in step 1). The width of the folds should be the same as the width of the angels, but the depth of the card needs to be at least 2 cm (¾ in) greater. Trim if necessary.

6

Use the glue stick to attach the angel cut-outs to the gold paper, carefully matching the fold lines. Re-fold the card to fit into an envelope.

Christmas candle

This glittery card shows how effective a repeat pattern can be. You could use this idea to create other card designs, such as Christmas trees, holly leaves or twinkling stars.

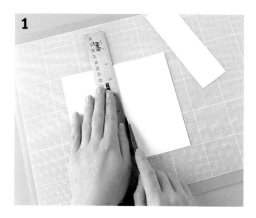

Mark out a rectangle 16 x 15 cm (6¼ x 6 in) in pencil on the white textured card, then cut out with the craft knife and metal ruler. With the longest edge at the top, score down the centre and fold. This is your card blank.

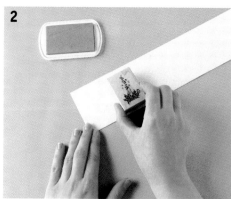

On the remaining white textured card, stamp a row of candles. You will barely be able to see the design as the ink is clear. Stamp more images than you need, as some may not be perfect.

3

Working quickly, fold a sheet of scrap paper in half, then open it out. Holding the stamped card over the scrap paper, sprinkle over the red embossing powder (you need to do this before the ink dries). Shake the excess powder back onto the paper, then tip it back into the pot.

4

Holding the stamped card with tweezers or tongs, heat the embossing powder with the heat tool (see page 12) until melted. Mark a pencil rectangle 5 x 3.5 cm (2 x 1¼ in) around each stamp, keeping the design central, and cut out.

5

Sprinkle gold glitter embossing powder onto the scrap paper. Working quickly, press each edge of the design into the side of the embossing stamp pad (this is where there is most ink).

6

Dip the edges of the card rectangle into the gold powder. Melt with the heat tool as before.

7

Measure out a rectangle 12 x 5.5 cm (4¾ x 2¼ in) on the sheet of red card and cut out.

8

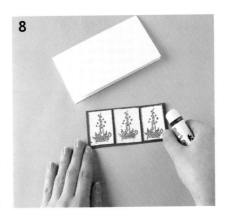

Glue three candle images onto the red card, then glue the red rectangle onto the white card blank.

The Christmas Table

The Christmas lunch or dinner table is an ideal place to display festive craft creations. Delight friends and family with homemade place settings that truly capture the spirit of the season. Sparkly napkins and candles create a celebratory atmosphere, while the luxury of lush candle rings with fruits and foliage will help make the meal really special.

Tabletop Christmas tree

It is hard to believe that when the life of the humble poppy is over, exotic and sculptural seedheads come from the same plant. As the most exciting part of the seedhead is the fabulous star-shaped tip, it is worth showing this off to its best advantage — a mini Christmas tree makes the perfect opportunity to do this, as the pretty stars all face outwards from a central cone.

1

You may be able to buy dry oasis in a small enough cone-shape, but generally, most cones are a little too large for this project and need to be pared down using a long-bladed kitchen knife. Remember that the poppy heads are quite large and will make the final shape a lot bigger than you might imagine. Experiment a little first if you're not sure. When you have a suitably sized, rough cone shape, paint it with a pale colour emulsion paint. Leave to dry.

2

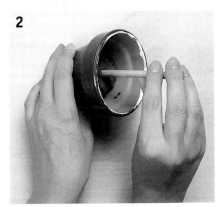

Paint the terracotta pot with the same emulsion paint to act as a primer then, when dry, coat with dark green gloss or enamel paint. Leave to dry. Squash some soft florist's clay into the base of the pot and cut down a piece of garden bamboo cane which will anchor the cone into the clay.

3

Sort the poppy heads into different sizes; the larger ones will form the base of the tree. Cut the poppy heads down so that the stems are really short (around 2.5 cm/1 in) and, to make it easier to insert them into the foam, cut them at an angle. Begin by slotting the larger seedheads in around the base of the tree, butting each one up to its neighbour.

4

Work up the tree, graduating the poppy heads, so that you begin with the larger ones and finish with the smaller ones at the top. For the neatest finish, work up the cone in straight lines from the base. Although it may not work exactly, you will achieve a more uniform finish. At this stage, you can swap about the seedheads to achieve the best effect, but once you are happy with the overall shape, remove the heads, one at a time, add a dab of glue and push back into the foam.

5

Use narrow strips of tartan ribbon and form into little bows. Wrap a piece of stub wire once around the centre of the bow, and twist the wire tails together to secure them. Add the bows to the tree at random. Give the whole tree a spray with the silver or clear glitter spray and finish with a little tartan ribbon wrapped around the pot.

Variations

You can use other seedheads for this project – Nigella, for example – or try the tiny pine cones available from most floral suppliers. These do not need to be wired into the foam, but instead can be stuck on with a glue gun. For a more glitzy effect, spray the whole tree with silver, gold or copper paint, then add ropes of pearls or glittering stars.

Pleated gold napkin

Ideal for a sparkly Christmas table setting, this particular fold works well on very fine or silky napkins, which show off the pleats to maximum effect. The tight pleats can be achieved with heavy starching and a hot iron.

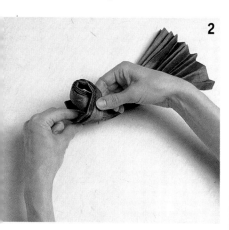

1 Starting at one edge, finely accordion pleat along the napkin's length, pressing firmly as you work along it.

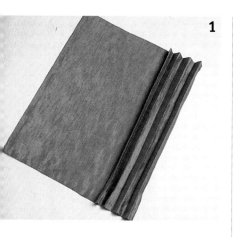

2 Make a knot at one end, leaving a short tail.

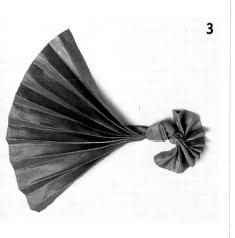

3 Finally, fan out the napkin and place it on the dinner plate.

Christmas tree napkin

This beautiful, elegant fold forms a tall, tree-like shape as the pleats are made diagonally across the napkin instead of the usual vertical pleats. The napkin should be thoroughly starched and stiff, so that it will stand upright without constantly toppling. It is made here in a pale colour so that the method of folding is clear, but try using a dark green napkin for a really festive effect.

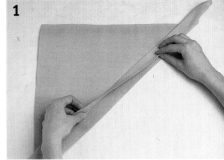

1 Fold the napkin in half diagonally, to form a triangle and begin to pleat from the widest part of the triangle.

2 Proceed to pleat the napkin, accordion fashion all along the triangular shape, pressing each pleat firmly with a hot iron as you do so. Complete the pleating when you reach the point of the triangle.

3 Fold the pleated napkin in half with the shortest side on the outside. Allow the longest parts of the napkin to meet and press firmly. The shortest end will act as a platform on which the fan will sit.

Candle ring

YOU WILL NEED

chicken wire
secateurs or wire cutters
wet florist's foam
gardening gloves
a few stub wires
stems of foliage
scissors
3-4 lemons
3-4 limes
cocktail or orange sticks
white daisy chrysanthemums
white spider chrysanthemums
floral candle holders
3 yellow candles

No special dinner would be complete without a spectacular centrepiece. Candles are a traditional favourite, and these tall yellow ones sit in a garland of shiny foliage, bright, crisp flower heads and mouthwatering lemons and limes. Candle rings are popular in many cultures, the circle signifying friendship. Although a fabulous piece, this candle ring should not take you more than an hour to put together. Remember, do not leave lit candles unattended.

1

Cut a long rectangle of chicken wire (this one was about 60 x 30 cm (24 x 12 in), although you can make this larger or smaller) and place small blocks of wet foam along its length, like a little train. Fold the wire lengthways into the centre, twisting the raw edges together to secure it. Wear the gloves when doing this as the wire is quite sharp.

2

Twist the wire and foam sausage into a circle, moulding it against your waist for a rounded effect. Join the two ends with some stub wires and adjust until you are happy with the circle. Begin to add short pieces of foliage, pushing the stem ends into the wet foam and working around the ring in one direction only.

3

When the wire is virtually covered both inside and out with foliage, add the fruit. These can be used whole or cut in half. Push each piece on to a cocktail or orange stick and push the stick firmly into the foam.

4

Add clusters of chrysanthemums into the arrangement, cutting their stems short and pushing them into the foam. Work around the circle in the same direction as the foliage.

5

Finally, add the candle holders. Floral candle holders have spikes so that you can push them into the foam. Set them around the ring, equidistantly and then pop the candles in place and light.

Tip

If you are unable to buy floral candle holders, buy plain flat ones, made either from glass or metal, and set them against the inner edges of the garland, tucking them well into the foliage so that the bases are covered.

Stamped candles

These festive candles will liven up the party table. They have been stamped with star designs using stamping paint. When stamping on wax, it is worth experimenting with different paints as some of them will not dry and just smudge. This technique can be used to make a range of inexpensive party table decorations; use the stamp to make matching napkins, napkin holders, or even a special tablecloth.

1 To make your potato stamp, take a potato (preferably one with a hard inner surface) and clean thoroughly. Cut it in half.

2 Draw a star shape onto the cut side of the potato using a felt-tipped pen.

3 Then, using a craft knife, carefully cut away the part of the design you do not want printed, so that the part you do want stands proud of the surface.

4 Finally, paint colour onto the stamp and test on a piece of paper before printing onto the candle surface. Gold, red and green are good colour choices for Christmas candles.